Here's what's b

How to be the Happies

by MARC MERO

"Marc Mero has a gift for capturing the readers attention and keeping it. His book is filled with great thoughts, scripture, life principles, illustrations, and challenges. Simple yet deep, this book provides real and practical ways to be a success in life. How to be the Happiest Person on the Planet offers a powerful, down-to-earth message that is attainable for all.

PASTOR TOM HERTWECK, Founding/Senior Pastor
Trinity Assembly of God in Clay, New York

"People of all ages and walks of life will find insightful gems of wisdom in Marc Mero's book. His life-changing message is presented in an entertaining way that motivates readers to make positive choices, use their God-given talents, and love like there's no tomorrow!"

MICHELE G. HUDSON, Arts & Entertainment Journalist
and Founder, www.TopofMindTalent.com

"I'm going to Think POZ everyday — NO — every minute of my life. This is going to be a best seller to those who take the time to read it. I love the practical POZ Pointers at the end of each chapter. Marc, you never cease to amaze me. Thank you for sharing your story!"

MIKE ANDRIANO, Senior Pastor
River Run Christian Church in Chuluota, Florida

"Marc Mero takes you on a journey of tragedy and triumph. The story of his personal life and professional career will touch your heart in such a way that it will never be the same. He will inspire you to reach your fullest potential and become a person of hope. Marc Mero is by far the happiest person on the planet!"

MICHAEL HENTY, author of *Go For God's Gold*

How to be the Happiest Person
on the Planet

God Bless

Think Poz !

Marc Mero

Goo Guss !
think poz !
NomNom :)

How to be the Happiest Person on the Planet

MARC MERO

How to be the Happiest Person
on the Planet

© 2011 by Marc Mero

Cover design: Tony Palmiotti

Cover photograph: Carlos A. Navarro
photographybynavarro.com

NEW EDUCATION PRESS
6137 East Mescal Street
Scottsdale, Arizona 85254

NewEducationPress.com

978-1-932842-56-2 — $ 15.95 — paperback

978-1-932842-57-9 — $ 15.95 — eBook

Printed in the United States of America

This book is dedicated to everyone who aspires to
live life to the fullest and make a difference in this world.
May you be inspired to Think POZ… Dream BIG…
live BOLDLY… give GENEROUSLY… laugh OFTEN
and LOVE eternally!

ACKNOWLEDGMENTS

This book would not be possible if not for the love and support of my wife Darlene, my "Pumpkin." What a perfect combination of love and laughter. I will always be grateful for your encouragement and enthusiasm as I pursue God's calling in my life. He couldn't have placed me with a better partner to enjoy this journey!

To my sister Jodi... I have watched you dedicate your life to saving and caring for animals. You have inspired me by your unselfish devotion to giving a voice to abused animals and making their lives so special. I never thought I would have three dogs!

To my brother Joel... I have watched you turn your life around through your faith in God. I read your daily writings to be blessed and inspired. Your amazing spirit has been such a motivational boost in my life.

A special thank you to my mother-in-law Gertie. One of the happiest days of our lives was when you moved in. I cherish our mornings together. I live with an angel — who's a great cook!

To my stepson Paul... Your dedication and love for your family is a privilege to watch and admire. You make us very proud.

To my mentor and the greatest man I know, Ray Rinaldi... I would need another book to write all the amazing things you do to help others. I am doing exactly what you taught me.

To my family members who have passed before me… My memories of you are etched in my heart. I have learned so much from each of you that I use in my everyday life. Mom, Dad, Guy and Andrea… you taught me about compassion, the value of family, and the importance of laughter. Most importantly you taught me to appreciate and respect life.

I want to thank Michael Henty for his wise counsel, support, and for his inspiration and friendship. Also a big thank you to Debbie Lynn Karl and Michele G. Hudson for their editorial assistance. Additionally, I extend my gratitude to Dr. Steven E. Swerdfeger with New Education Press for his commitment to excellence throughout this publishing project.

FOREWORD
by Diamond Dallas Page

$\mathcal{I}$ remember it like it was yesterday. I was sitting in the World Championship Wrestling (WCW) TV Production room watching Ron Simmons wrestle an unknown enhancement opponent when former Hall of Fame pro wrestler "The American Dream" Dusty Rhodes said, "Dallas ... Whooo's Dat kid? ... Dat kid's got Somthin!"

That was the day Marc Mero, or "Double M" as I like to call him, got his big break. That was also the day Marc Mero got his first opportunity to live out his childhood dream and went on to become a Wrestling Champion.

Over the next few years I would go on to share many miles, memories, and matches with Marc. Oh boy, those matches... Ha! We were both green as grass in the ring back then, but we truly brought out the best in each other.

It's been over 20 years now and Marc is still one of my very closest friends. I've had the privilege of watching Marc go though a personal transformation. You see, Marc has somewhat of an addictive personality. To say his life has been a bit of a Roller Coaster may be an understatement.

Marc shares many of his personal struggles and triumphs in his book, *How to be the Happiest Person on the Planet.* He wrote this book to help others — to encourage people he doesn't even know to find their way, and to inspire them to achieve a Positive Attitude.

The best part of having an addictive personality is when you finally get addicted to Health, Happiness and Helping others. That's when you realize what life is truly all about. Marc's life is now dedicated to making a difference using these principles.

i

Throughout this book, Marc leads you by example as he lives life with a Positive Attitude! And he wants to help YOU do the same! Once Marc embraced his POZ Attitude I knew he was well on his way to Changing the World and making it a better place. He's not just saying he's the "Happiest Person on the Planet" ... He really, Really, REALLY means it, and his infectious attitude can help you do the same!

Trust me. I know a little something about being POSITIVE:)

Diamond Dallas Page
3-time World Champion Wrestler
Fitness Guru, Inspirational Speaker
Actor and Author of the book *Positively Page*

Introduction

The first thing you should know about me is that I am the self-proclaimed "happiest person on the planet." The second thing you should know about me is that's not always been the case. I was best known for playing the flamboyant characters Johnny B. Badd in World Championship Wrestling (WCW), and Wildman Marc Mero and Marvelous Marc Mero with World Wrestling Entertainment (WWE). I wrestled for almost 14 years, traveling the world to as many as 250 cities annually.

I have been through some pretty bad times and made some really bad decisions. Even though I was once a sports champion in wrestling, boxing, football and hockey, I haven't always been a "champion of choices." But today is a new day for me...

My life is transformed — thanks to a newfound faith in God, new family and friends, and an incredible wife! In the last seven years,

WWE Intercontinental Champion

I've gone from believing the worst will happen, to believing the best will happen. I've gone from waiting for things to happen, to making things happen. I've gone from being addicted to drugs, to now being addicted to happiness.

1

I know it sounds a little "out there," but I'm truly hooked on happiness. I can't get enough of making other people smile, of helping others see a way out of the darkness, and of being thankful for the great things in life. Happiness is a choice. Every day, I love life... I love God... I love my wife. I love my family, my friends and my pets. I also love you, my readers. When you're a happy person you naturally care about others; there's no such thing as a stranger.

I have lived for half a century now, and I see different ways people respond to hardship and loss. The same tragedy that makes one person better makes another person bitter. So what is the difference? The difference is choice! The choice to seek happiness, feel it, and share it with others.

Success is not the key to happiness; happiness is the key to success!

Before I accepted God in my life and decided to think positively, I confused the order of success and happiness. I thought that if I were successful — had the money, the fame, the big house, the pretty girls, the shiny car — then I'd be happy. I had it all wrong. Today I realize that if you are happy — with family, friends, and faith — then you are successful. I made a lot of mistakes. I lost a lot of friends. And I suffered a lot of despair.

If you get one thing out of this book, I hope it's the realization that it's not too late to have hope for a happier tomorrow, no matter how miserable yesterday may have been.

You are in control of your own destiny.

This book offers my thoughts on how to become the happiest person on the planet. Some of us believe that happiness is for the afterlife and, while we are here on earth, we are destined to suffer. I have found this notion farthest from the truth. Put your faith and trust in

God's hands and your life will change. Happiness is a choice. If you want to be the happiest person on the planet, begin with these nine choices.

Each of these choices is a chapter in my book:

1. Think "POZ" (Positive).
2. Dream BIG.
3. Live in the moment.
4. Make someone's day.
5. Surround yourself with POZ people.
6. Let it go.
7. Do the right thing.
8. Get back up.
9. Believe the best is yet to come.

You are in control of your own destiny.

Try some of the helpful hints (POZ Pointers) at the end of each chapter. Start by believing great things are in store for you and that God has a purpose for your life.

With faith in God and positive thinking, you too can be the happiest person on the planet. Now give me a BIG smile. Feels good, doesn't it?

Chapter One: Think POZ!

On your mark, get set, smile. Is it that easy? It can be.

𝑅emember the song "Hakuna Matata" in Disney's film *The Lion King*? It's actually a Swahili phrase that is literally translated as "There are no worries."

> *"Whether you think you can or you can't, you're right."*
> HENRY FORD

The expression was made famous by a meerkat and a warthog. While the phrase carried a slight implication of a complete lack of ambition, what these characters were really suggesting is that a lion cub named Simba should forget his troubled past and live in the present. In other words, they were teaching him to "Think POZ." Great advice. No wonder the Elton John hit was nominated for Best Original Song at the 1995 Academy Awards. Cartoons aside, we are blessed with a free will, and that includes choices.

We need to learn how to be positive. "Think POZ." By this I mean to be positive in accord with God's plan and purpose. But how do you know what that is? The Bible speaks much wisdom. According to the Gospel of Mark (verse 11:23), the will of God is for us to say it with our mouth and believe it in our heart. *"I tell you the truth, if anyone says to this mountain, 'Go, throw yourself into the sea,' and does not doubt in his heart but believes that what he says will happen, it will be done for him."* That's faith! Faith and positive thinking go hand in hand.

Attitude is a choice. If you think positive thoughts, you get positive results. It's that simple. All you have to do is choose. Start out each day by saying; I'm going to have a great day.

Then go and do something special for someone.

I'm deeply thankful for so many things in my life. It's easy to be thankful because I choose to believe life is great. I have a wonderful wife, a beautiful home, an unbelievably supportive family, and good friends. It all started with a new and improved outlook on life — a renewed faith in God and a belief that he has a purpose for each of us. I want to accomplish His purpose and be a positive example of how happy and fulfilling life can be by doing the right things and choosing the right attitude.

Happiest Couple

Every day, I choose to be happy. I choose to "Think POZ."

Now, it needs to be said that just because you think positive thoughts doesn't mean negative things won't happen. We all face adversity, whether it's as small as a flat tire or as significant as the loss of a loved one. Are you dealing with disappointment, stress, defeat? It's easy to feel hopeless; we've all been there.

When this happens, the alternative is to focus less on the situation itself and more on your reaction to it. Again, it's all about the attitude. Thinking positive thoughts can lead to positive outcomes.

Let's put this thinking to the test. Assess your attitude right now. Consider the following setbacks and reflect on how you would react if this happened to you. Be honest.

> Stuck in a traffic jam
> Your dog runs away
> Lost your homework
> Late for work
> Not enough money to buy gas
> A quarrel with a parent, or sibling

For each of the above, what's your attitude? Are you feeling frustrated? Irritated? Discouraged?

Now, consider your responses to the following lists of setback.

> In a car accident
> Your dog dies
> Lost your home
> Fired from your job
> Not enough money to buy food
> The death of a parent or sibling

The hardships got worse, right? Now, how are you feeling? Sad? Victimized? Hopeless? This list puts the first set of troubles in perspective, does it not?

Perhaps you have experienced some of the challenges above. Some of you may have had to bear most or all of them. If so, you and I have something in common. I've endured everything on both lists. In later chapters, I'll share my stories, but just understand that I know what it feels like to lose a family member. My sister Andrea died when she was only 21; my mother and brother died only two weeks apart; and my father died in my arms. I also know what it feels like to lose a friend — over 30 of them, and lose a home — we moved eight times and I attended eight schools before I graduated high school.

Sister Andrea

Many of us have had our world turned upside down. Life is not always the way we think it should be or the way we want it to be. I know many of your life challenges because you share them with me. I receive over a hundred e-mails and letters each week from families that have seen my **Champion of Choices** program in schools, churches, and youth organizations in the USA and across the globe.

John, age 13, wrote: *You were talking about good choices at our school today and you pulled out a "Death List" about everyone you knew and cared about who had died. I thought you might like to hear this story: A couple of weeks before you came to our school I found out my cousin Billy was going to die in a matter of days. My cousin is not even two years old. That isn't much of a life, is it? My mom is crying and my grandma is heartbroken. All through this, I never cried a tear. After you came and talked at our school, I thought about it all day. As soon as I got home, I started crying. You really helped me finally break through that numbness I felt and I let the tears fall.*

You really inspired me and I want to thank you for making me realize I can be a Champion for Billy. I was not allowed to stay after the ceremony so I did not get an autograph. I was wondering if you could send me an autograph in the mail so I could cheer up my dad because he got me into wrestling and is a big fan.

7

"The Billy thing" is really hitting him hard, but he's still trying to make me believe everything's okay. I am not good at sports and I have an awkward physique, but I will be a wrestling champion who started out small, just like you. My first match will be for Billy. Maybe you'll be in the audience watching me.

Jackie, age 15, wrote: *First off let me start by saying you're a great inspiration. With all that you've been through, it's great that you can hold your head up so high. I saw you at our School today. Wow… your story was amazing. I realized my confidence level isn't the best. I feel like an outcast at my school [because of my ADHD and OCD]. I feel that these issues hold me back. But if you can reach your goals, I can too.*

You've also made me realize that when my six-year-old sister is all excited to see me, I shouldn't just walk by. And she always asks me to play, but I always make up an excuse because I don't want too. But I know I will regret it someday, so I'll take every chance I get to hang out with my little sister. Thank you so much.

Some of our greatest opportunities are a result of our greatest disappointments.

Believe it or not, the way we deal with affliction makes all the difference. So when bad things happen to you, don't look to the heavens and shout, why me? If you keep thinking positive, you'll discover there was a purpose to your pain. Inevitably, the silver lining is right around the corner. In Romans 8:28 we read: *"And we know that in all things God works for the good of those who love him, who have been called according to his purpose."*

The world can be a dark place, but with the right attitude, you can light it as much as needed. Your attitude and a faith in better things to come is your source of light. Choosing to "Think POZ" is your remedy. When you feel hopeless, happiness seems impossible. I remember times in my life when I didn't think things could get any worse. When I lost my family, I never felt so low. I didn't want to go on and face another day. But you have to believe things will get better. Remember, too, it's one thing to say you choose to "Think POZ;" it's another thing to really be aware of your thoughts and behaviors and make sure you are replacing negative thoughts with hope.

No matter how bad things are in your life right now, believe it will get better. I promise it will. I never thought I could endure all the hardships and losses I suffered, but I did. God will walk with you through every trial, hardship and challenge. The Bible says that our works will be tried by fire. I also look at our life as being tried by fire — and a series of "tests." Wood, hay, and little sticks burn up in a fire, but precious stones will endure forever. You are a precious stone and you have to believe that!

Happiness is a choice.

You can change your life by changing your attitude. I know this because I did it. I don't want to take away from the fact that my faith helped me through some rough times… I give all glory and honor to God. My attitude change has had a huge impact on my happiness, my relationships, and how I deal with adversity, big or small. While I used to feel like a victim, I now think like a victor. While I used to think the worst would happen, I now believe the best will happen. In other words, my glass is now "half full," not "half empty." To be truthful, as the happiest person on the planet, I look at my glass as overflowing!

In a way, "Thinking POZ" is a responsibility. It's about taking ownership for your responses to what life brings you. Whether we are adults or children, learning we have control over our attitude is essential to our happiness. We can either give in to external events and pressures — few of which we can control — or we can take control of our outlook.

"I just want to be happy." I hear it all the time. Many people aren't happy with their lives because they think something else out there creates happiness rather than choosing it for themselves. Many people fall for "the grass is greener elsewhere syndrome." Let me set the record straight: the grass is not greener over here or over there; the grass is greenest where you water it!

There is an old saying: **Happiness is like a butterfly which, when pursued, is always beyond our grasp; but, if you will sit down quietly, it will land upon you.**

Embrace what you already have. It's unfortunate I had to lose it all before I finally found what is truly important.

We can't control our economy or our environment, but we can control what we do and think. At **Marc Mero Body Slam**, my gym in Central Florida, we have a slogan: **Change your mind, change your body, change your life!** I changed my mind by changing my attitude. I changed my body by putting my faith in God and seeing my body as a temple. I changed my life by becoming hooked on happiness. I now have healthy thoughts, healthy habits, and a healthy attitude. With these three things, my life has been revived.

In time, thinking positive does become easier. Once you change your attitude, you start to feel better, little by little. When you adjust your outlook — to see clear sky through the clouds — staying positive takes less effort. Remember, after every storm, the sun does eventually come out! "Thinking POZ" becomes a habit. Take it from me... someone who embraced change and is now hooked on happiness.

Happiness is a gift.

The choice of a positive attitude is one of the few things this world cannot take away from us. We own it. And once you realize you have this personal power, you will improve how you react to situations. Negative attitudes get in the way of goals and relationships. Positive attitudes bring energy, results and healthy relationships.

For many of us, the toughest time to "Think POZ" is during the holidays. Take Christmas for example. Maybe it's been a difficult year, and when the holidays roll around, you feel the blues more than ever. A time meant to bring joy, good tidings, and time spent with loved ones may instead bring sadness and despair. If your troubles stem from broken relationships or the loss of one near and dear, feelings of loneliness can be more amplified during Christmas. You begin to think negative thoughts. I know this too well.

When I lost so many family members and friends, I remember the solitude of Christmas day. I remember sitting alone under a pier at Cocoa Beach, Florida, thinking the worst possible thoughts. I didn't want to be here... I wasn't sure I wanted to go on living. I just watched the waves roll in and out, believing the end was near. Did you ever feel so empty, unwanted, and alone?

When this happens, you must find peace within yourself. Besides the magnificent gift of God's Son Jesus, Christmas bears the gift of peace. Search within your heart for that inner peace, and the gift of happiness will come too. Also bear in mind that God gave us each a special talent. Use that talent to do good things that bring joy to you and to others. This is the utmost gift that needs to be unwrapped, treasured, and shared.

What gifts are you overlooking right now? What new ritual can you start that brings peace and happiness to you and "transmits" joy to others?

When I come home from the office at night, my family sees me happy. "Hi Pumpkin!" (my wife Darlene)… "Hi Matka!" (Polish for Mommy, my Mother-in-law)…"Hi Paul!" (My stepson). Our three dogs Kato, Maui and Rocco come running to my arms. Hugs and kisses all around. This is our ritual. This is my gift of happiness. I look forward to it every day.

Maui

In the past, my ritual was to arrive home, walk in and ask, "Is dinner ready?"… Are the bills paid?"… "What is this mess?" I have exchanged demands for demonstrations of love. I changed from negative expectations to positive ones. I choose to be happy. Each day is a gift, not a given. How will you use it?

Happiness is now.

Don't wait on happiness. Don't make the mistake of putting off happiness for the weekend, or the next vacation. And don't wait for a new year to change your attitude. When someone asks: "How are you today?" and you respond with "Good" — that's okay; but what happens when you respond with "Great!" It puts you further ahead than just "Good."

Kato

Sometimes, days, months and years go by and you might still find yourself saying: "I want to change." Don't procrastinate! "Think POZ." And don't try and change everybody else. Instead, change yourself and wait for the magic to occur. You will attract positive people and positive outcomes.

While we cannot choose what happens to us, we can choose what happens *"in"* us. Choose the right attitude — one in which you view challenges as opportunities instead of problems.

Life holds wonderful things for you. Don't let circumstances — or negative people — tell you otherwise. Don't let yourself become fooled into believing life doesn't hold great things. You have to believe! You become what you think. Expect good things. Expect them today. Every day starts with a new choice. What attitude are you choosing today?

POZ Pointers

❖ **Write down three positive thoughts.**
❖ **Create a ritual that can bring happiness to you and to others.**
❖ **Focus more on what you have, not on what you think you need.**

Chapter Two: DREAM Big!

Seeing isn't believing; believing is seeing.

There is no better testament to this than the faith and actions of Ray, the character played by Kevin Costner in the 1989 film, *Field of Dreams*. While walking through his cornfield, Ray, a farmer in rural Iowa, hears a voice whisper, "If you build it, they will come." Ray has a vision of a baseball field. In spite of the skepticism of his neighbors and family, Ray plows his corn and builds the field. He has a dream, and he makes it happen.

Everyone needs something to believe in, something they can whole-heartedly be enthusiastic about. Life has more meaning when you work toward something that is important to you, and do what it takes to make it happen. Dreams not only give you a purpose and a reason to get up in the morning; they can keep you going all day. Dreams allow you to draw the best out of life. And if you are going to dream, you might as well dream BIG! While goals need to be realistic and within your reach in the foreseeable future, dreams need to be slightly beyond your current grasp.

> *"So many of our dreams at first seem impossible, then they seem improbable, and then when we summon the will, they soon become inevitable."*
> **CHRISTOPHER REEVE**

As the famous song promises: *somewhere over the rainbow, skies are blue... and the dreams that you dare to dream really do come true.* What is your dream?

When I was a young boy I had this amazing dream of being rich and famous. I wanted to be a professional athlete, and not only that, I wanted to win "Rookie of the Year." Once I set my sights on these dreams, all my actions went toward making them come true. I worked and trained hard and told myself and others: "I can do this."

Dream Big!

My pursuit began at 11 years old when I decided to try out for hockey. I couldn't skate, and all

Goalie 1972

the other players made fun of me because I could barely stand up on my skates. I was so inept I had to play goalie, and I wasn't very good at all.

Every practice, I stayed after and worked on my goaltending.

I went home to our apartment and I would practice every day with my brother Joel. I imagined myself blocking shots, making save after save. I wasn't going to give up the dream. By the end of that year, our team had played 20 games; and of those 20 games, I had 13 shutouts, meaning no one scored a goal on me in 13 of the 20 games. Our team

15

won the championship and I was voted the league's "Most Valuable Player."

The following summer, I dedicated myself and learned how to skate. And the next season I played center and led the league in scoring. My sophomore year in high school I played varsity and led my team in scoring. By my senior year, I became first team all-county in both hockey and football.

Liverpool High School 1979

It was also in high school that I discovered the sport I thought would fulfill my dream of making me "rich and famous." I was with some friends and we passed by a Boxing poster ad for the New York State Golden Gloves. When I stopped and pointed at it, one of my buddies said: "You want to go watch that?" And I said, "Go watch it; I want to enter it and win the title! I can do that!"

Did you ever get that "Ah-ha" moment where you see something or somebody do something and you say to yourself: "I can do that!" My friends said: "Marc, are you crazy? Those guys will knock you out." (You are going to meet a lot of negative people along your path to success. Don't let them derail you if you feel your dream is God inspired.)

So, I set to work chasing the dream. I knew of a local gym where they trained boxers, and I went every day to learn and pursue my dream. I met my mentor and boxing coach, Ray Rinaldi, who became like a second father to me. I learned so much from that man; I still do! And guess what? I won the whole state of New York.

Believing is the first step to achieving!

In spite of many setbacks, what kept my sights high was my belief. At the time, I didn't have God in my life, so my faith was more in myself — my own abilities and perseverance. I also found strength in someone else's confidence in me — my mom's. The greatest gift my mother Dianne gave me was her belief in me. She made me feel like I could do anything.

New York State Boxing Champion with Father "Happy" Mero and Coach Ray Rinaldi

This was particularly special because growing up, we were very poor. My mom worked two jobs while my older sister Jodi took care of us. We didn't have much, but we had each other. My mother taught me to dream, to dream big and never give up on a better future, no matter how unlikely the circumstances of the present.

Apartment we grew up in

With my mother's encouragement, I dreamed of a better life. With my positive attitude, I believed it could happen. With my determination, I took action toward the dream. But there was one more factor that led to my dreams coming true... **I wrote them into existence.**

At 10 years old, I started writing down my dreams and goals. For example, I once got a ride home from school in my friend's father's

First house and new Cadiillac

black Cadillac. When I got home, I wrote down in my little notebook that I wanted a fancy Cadillac one day. When I made it big in wrestling, guess which car I first bought myself? That's right, a brand new black Cadillac! I still drive one to this day! On the little television we owned, I once saw a commercial with a guy driving a speedboat. I said to myself, "Wow, I want one of those one day," and I wrote it down. Guess what is docked in my backyard today?

It was on this same tiny TV set that I would watch sports. I loved football, hockey, boxing, wrestling and basketball. I would imagine myself running plays and commentating. *Pass over to Mero, five seconds left in the game; Knicks are down by one. Mero fades left; fades right; here's the shot! Three-Two-One... It's in! Marc Mero just won the NBA championship of the world for the New York Knicks!* This is where the dreams for becoming a pro athlete and winning "Rookie of the Year" began. I wrote my goals down. Then I took action and watched my dreams come true.

Twenty-one years later, I did win "Rookie of the Year" as voted by the fans of *Pro Wrestling Illustrated*. It was a big dream, but I had taken action toward it one step at a time.

As adults, many of us stop dreaming. Why? Because it takes courage to dream big. As a grown-up, it might seem silly or frivolous to think about dreams. If you were to mention your dreams to someone, they might tell you to "get real." Yet I meet adults that will say, "I wish I would have done this or done that." My response is, *so what's stopping you?*

What tends to happen in life is that we fall into a routine, and then "the usual" carries us through life. We begin to settle for the status quo. We quit setting goals. Then before we know it, ten years have gone by and we regret that we haven't accomplished as much as we had once expected. *We feel disappointed and wonder where did the time go? What happened?* What happened was this — we stopped dreaming. We quit taking risks. We stopped believing in ourselves.

We miss 100% of the shots we don't take.

The greatest risk in life is not taking one, *so go for it!* Dreams never die, only the dreamer does. Don't let life pass you by without giving it your best shot. It's never too late to become what you might have been. Take my wife for example. She always dreamed of having her own company.

Starting from her dining room table in 1995 with limited inventory and funds, Darlene Spezzi had a dream of creating a dynamic and unique company. Scraping together investment money, Darlene began laying the foundation of her dream, which today is known as **Mystic Granite and Marble**. In the beginning, sales were slow. With no delivery truck, customers had to pick up their own orders. It seemed that

Mystic Granite & Marble

19

the dream was impossible. Yet with hard work and dedication, sales soon reached a half a million dollars.

Darlene invested in more advertising and marketing and visited potential customers with new products. She also splurged and bought a red delivery truck. Keeping her eye on the dream, Darlene continued to listen to the needs of the Orlando market as home construction started to boom. It was the beginning of the "stone age" when granite and marble's popularity began to surge in Central Florida. Now her company is one of the area's most successful distributors of natural stone in tile and slab. She had a dream… she believed… and she took action!

I meet people who dream about becoming professional dancers, speakers, athletes, scientists, you name it. I had dreams as a young boy, and I still have dreams as an adult. The goals themselves may be different now, but they're still dreams with merit that deserve our exploration. And I still write them down. (In fact, I still have the little "dream book" that I kept as a child.)

Today, my desk is covered with post-it notes, each one representing a goal. There's a famous Harvard study which shows that writing down goals significantly increases the chance of achieving them. Consider this as proof: For two years, I had a post-it on my computer that stated, "Write a book." And with prayer and perseverance you are reading my realized dream.

> *"The future belongs to those who believe in the beauty of their dreams."*
> ELEANOR ROOSEVELT

Don't ever stop dreaming!

Research tells us that besides writing down their dreams, people who *dream* big *win* big; they make a commitment to do so, and are relentless in their pursuit. They set goals and take action toward those goals. And they aren't afraid to fail.

I once heard of a high-school math instructor issuing a challenge at a school assembly: "I hope you all fail." Harsh as it sounded, he said it to an audience of high-school seniors eager to go out and conquer the world. He then added, "Because, if you don't, you haven't set your goals high enough," meaning if you don't falter a few times, you never achieve your greatest potential. Michelangelo gave us this to think about: **Failure is not aiming high and missing; failure is aiming too low and hitting.**

21

You have to believe in yourself, and you can't be afraid to fail a few times along the way. There is amazing power in acting as if something has already happened. Trust me on this one; you have within you the strength to change the world. You just have to believe.

5 Steps to Dreaming BIG

1. **Write Them Down** — Placing dreams and goals in front of you helps you take action toward them.
2. **Aim High** — The bigger we allow ourselves to dream, the more we accomplish and the more we start to see what is possible.
3. **Spend Time** — Commit to making your dream happen. It's not going to magically materialize. It will take time and dedication, not just talking about it or wishing it into existence.
4. **Take Action Toward Your Dream** — I have found that many successful people leave a trail of success. Find someone who has done it before and seek out their wise counsel.
5. **Prayer** — Ask God to give you the strength, guidance, conviction and determination to make your dream a reality.

The real secret to dreaming BIG is finding a passion, doing what you love, and believing that in at least trying, it will make your soul rich. When you find your passion you never have to work! I often joke with my wife that at the end of the day I say "I'm on my way home from passion." I just can't call it work because I love what I do!

I not only found my passion, I found my life calling. It was June of 2007. I was reading online about a friend and fellow wrestler named Chris Benoit, who strangled his wife and smothered his seven-year-old son. He then hanged himself... his body found lifeless in his workout room.

When I read this, my life as I knew it changed. I was so tired of seeing and hearing about people in the wrestling industry dying — mostly due to their destructive choices — and wondered why something wasn't being done, that I decided to take action and do something.

I became a regular on national television shows like Nancy Grace, Glen Beck, Montel Williams, FOX, and CNN, shedding light on issues such as steroid-and prescription-drug abuse in the wrestling industry.

I also realized I wanted to make a difference in students' lives, instilling healthy habits and positive choices. So I founded my program called **Champion of**

Montel Williams Show

Choices and began presenting it at schools, churches, and corporations.

The goal of Champion of Choices is to offer opportunities for youth to participate in imaginative, motivational learning experiences that will assist them in building positive life skills, such as character education. These skills will enable them to make meaningful choices and to pursue their passions. This, in turn, promotes the healthy

23

development of America's youth, by affording them a resilient foundation through which to strengthen their families.

Erma Bombeck once wrote, "There are people who put their dreams in a little box and say, 'Yes, I've got dreams, of course I've got dreams.' Then they put the box away and bring it out once in awhile to look in it, and yep, they're still there. There are great dreams, but they never even get out of the box."

Don't keep your dreams in a box. Take them out and believe in them. Write them into existence and take action toward them today.

POZ Pointers

❖ Imagine yourself in that place of success.
❖ Believe in your heart you can accomplish anything you set your mind to.
❖ Write it down… write it into existence.
❖ Ask God to guide you along on your journey.

Chapter Three: Live in the moment.

The best way to appreciate what you have is to imagine yourself without it.

Do you remember when poor Rudolph's red nose was discovered and he was consequently banished by all the other reindeer? Discouraged, he wanders off into the woods, and empathetic Clarice follows him. She tells him not to worry that his nose is different because that's what makes it "grand." Then, as you would expect in early-day animated features, she sweetly breaks into song. She croons a few lines from Janet Orenstein's original hit: *There's always tomorrow for dreams to come to true.*

While a nice sentiment on Clarice's part, it's not always the case. Tomorrow does not always come. For Rudolph, sure, tomorrow does come; he gets the girl, the social acceptance, and the lead position in Santa's lineup. But that's fantasy. And this is real life. In real life, there isn't always the next day...or the next hour... or the next moment. I have seen this happen many times and know it to be true. Unfortunately, while God often gives us a second chance, sometimes it's not His will for tomorrow to come. In just minutes, even seconds, life can change. And change can be dramatic, even permanent.

Because we never know if there is going to be a tomorrow, don't wait to take action toward your dreams. Appreciate today. Savor every moment. And most importantly, enjoy the little things because one day you will look back and realize those were the big things.

It's true that we don't know what we've got until we lose it. I never realized this more than when I lost some of the most important people in my life — my mother, my brother, my sister, over 30 friends, and my father, who was my best friend. My wife walked out on me after almost

My father, Harold "Happy" Mero

ten years of marriage. Faced with these losses, I hit rock bottom. I didn't want to be here anymore. I knew how hard it would be without my family at Christmas, birthdays and Thanksgiving. Not even a phone call ever again. I had never felt this low. And let me tell you why. It wasn't just the notion that I would never see them again; it was the fact that while they were here, I never appreciated them.

My younger brother Guy looked up to me. From the time he was old enough to walk until I moved away from home, he always wanted me to play with him. He loved baseball, and always wanted me to pitch to him. I can remember him begging me to throw the ball to him, and I would say, "Go away you little punk." When he wouldn't give up, I'd take his ball and throw it as far away as I could. What I would give to have one more chance to pitch that ball to him.

My brother Guy

Be kind to each other. Hug more, kiss more and always say three simple words: "I love you!"

My little sister, Andrea looked up to me too. Whenever we would go somewhere together as a family, she'd always yell, "I want to sit next to Marc! I call it!" meaning that because she "called it" I had to sit by her. *This used to drive me crazy! Why did she have to sit right next to me? Why did she have to call it?* Now that's she's gone, what I would give to have a chance to sit next to her again.

I can't remember ever telling Andrea that I loved her. Why is it that so many of us have trouble with those words? I don't any more. I say "I love you" all the time now. They are my favorite words!

When we make bad choices, the people we hurt the most are the ones that love us the most.

Here's a real example that I look back on with regret. Whenever I used to come in from hanging out with my friends, my mother would wait up for me to make sure that I was safe. It was during a time I was making some pretty bad choices, and I would come in late after hours of drinking and doing drugs. I'd always see the light on in our window and know that Mom was up, knitting and waiting.

To avoid any confrontation, I'd head straight for my room when I walked through the door. But always, she would stop me and ask, "Marc, how was your night?" And I'd quickly respond with, "Fine, I'm just tired and want to go to bed."

Then she'd say, "But, Son, I haven't seen you all day; why don't you sit down and talk to me a few minutes," and I'd repeat, "No, I just want to go to bed." To her third request, I'd slam my door, and yell, "I just want to go to bed! Leave me alone!" This is how I treated the person who loved me and believed in me the most.

I remember the shocking moment I got the bad news about her death. I was wrestling in Hiroshima, Japan, one of many stops on a

My mom, Dianne, our last picture

worldwide wresting tour. After my match, I went back to my hotel and fell asleep. During the middle of the night, I got a knock on the door from the Japanese promoter who told me that I needed to call home because there was an emergency. When I called home, a family member said, "Marc, I don't know how to tell you this…" I said, "Just tell me." "Marc, I can't tell you… I don't know how." Then I yelled, "Just tell me!" She said, "Marc, your mother died."

How could this possibly be happening? Bad things weren't supposed to happen to a guy like me — a guy who "had it all" — the fancy cars, the wild parties, the famous friends, and the big houses. I was in my prime; I was successful. I was rich, I was famous, I was happy. Or so I thought.

Shaken by the news, I just dropped the phone and remember running through the hotel lobby and out into the street and shouting to the heavens, "I'm so sorry, Mom!" Here I was traveling around, drinking, doing drugs, making bad choices… and the person I owed the most to in life — the one who worked two jobs to keep us going, who taught me to live right and stay off drugs and out of gangs — was gone. It felt like a part of me died that day.

Even though I had eventually blessed her with a new home and grew to cherish the times we spent together, I was still *making bad choices*. If only my mom — my hero — could see me now, making good choices and helping others do the same. I had slammed the door and left her sitting there alone knitting, loving me unconditionally when I didn't deserve it. What I would give for one more chance just to sit and talk… to tell her how my day was and ask about hers.

I was on a wild ride when my mother died, obsessed with making more and more money. Sure, I had the money, the fame, and the fortune. I was so worried about making a living, I'd forgotten to make a life. Many people look to drugs, alcohol, or immorality for "happiness." They miss the true beauty and fulfillment their own family or friends can provide. They don't realize that happiness is right here, right now.

We tend to forget that happiness doesn't come as a result of getting something we don't have, but rather in recognizing and appreciating what we do have. That's the point I was missing. While flying across the world for my mother's funeral, for the first time in my life I finally realized what was most important. Family. And now it was too late.

I recall walking into the funeral home and seeing her casket in the distance. I remember the sick feeling I had inside. I just started praying, "Please wake up, Mom, please get up." As I walked closer to her casket, I could see that she was dressed in white. She looked like an angel. She was beautiful. I said, "Mom, you are my hero; everything I am, everything I hoped to be was because of you. You gave me life… you sacrificed to provide and care for us. Mom, you were the only one to believe in me; you loved me so much." And how had I repaid her? By getting drunk, by getting high, by hanging out with losers, and by becoming the biggest loser of all. I'm so sorry! As I write this it's hard to put into words the pain I am feeling.

If you appreciate someone, don't keep it a secret.

Instead, tell those closest to you what they mean to you. Tell them you love them. You might assume they know you love them, so you very seldom say the words. You think, *I'll tell them tomorrow.* But you might not get that chance. Make a commitment today to let your loved ones know how you feel, and tell them how special they are. Show your appreciation in both your words and your actions.

Every day I say, "I love you."

One of the greatest gifts you can give is that of attention. Sometimes we take for granted the very things that most deserve our gratitude. So offer that hug, make that phone call, write that e-mail, send that card, or look that special someone in the eye and let them know you truly love them. Instead of surfing the internet, interact with your family. Instead of sitting in front of the television, sit next to your sister and talk. Instead of throwing away your life, throw the ball.

I share this message with people like you all around the world. And what a difference it's making for those who listen. Brittany, a young teenager, has gone from constantly yelling at her six younger siblings to telling them she cares about them. "Today I came home," she writes to me, "and just grabbed my sister in my arms and told her I loved her. It felt weird, but amazing all at the same time."

Morgan, a high school student in New York shared after attending a Champion of Choices session: "I now realize that what others think does not matter and I should focus on making the ones I love happy… and I realize that no matter how mean my parents seem to me, they are doing it out of love. You have helped me realize that I should cherish my parents, for I never know when something could happen where I never see them again."

Touched by the same presentation, Kaylah shares, "I connected with your story about you not throwing the baseball to your brother, then he passed away. I am going to hang out with my little brother a lot more now and be nicer."

Gabrielle hugged her little brother when he got in from school and even though he rolled his eyes and said "whatever," she believes it made a positive impact!

Terry touched my heart with his following note:

> *Mr. Mero, your presentation today at Liverpool High School really inspired me to be a better person. I don't have the best relationship with my family, and I'm emotionally detached from them… I hardly ever have a pleasant conversation with my parents. Today, I came home and gave them a hug and told them how sorry I was for the way I had treated them. I went out of my way to be nice to my sister too. Life is too short to waste on anger and resentment. Sometimes it takes significant loss to realize that. It's true. You make mistakes. But what*

separates the boys from the men are the choices we make
after we mess up. Thanks for coming to our school.

Jackie posted on Facebook: "When I got home I did everything
with with my little sister and I said I'm never gunna be mean to you
again. And then I called my mom at work and said 'I love you' and she
was like, 'What's wrong with you?' I cried and told her thanks for being
there for me and that she was doing a great job raising us kids."

Tim went home that same day and told his sister she was the best.

The list goes on, and it's not just young people. Adam, a teacher
from Orlando said:

> *During your speech I snuck up behind my daughter Bella,*
> *and wrapped her in my arms, barely holding back my*
> *tears. I began teaching at her school so I could see her every*
> *day and have more "moments" since she lives with her*
> *mother. Holding her in my arms and listening to you talk*
> *was one of the biggest moments we've had these past three*
> *years. Thank you for providing that, Marc.*

John, a father and husband, was inspired by my lessons to spend
more time with his son Anthony, and heed his wife's and son's request
to stop drinking so much. Although he had to work hard to fight the
temptation and demons within, he is sticking to his commitment. Life
is just too short.

If you found out you had only one week to live, how would you spend it?

And when you take your final breath in this life, what will you truly cherish? It will never be how much money you had, how many A's you earned, or how popular you were. Instead, you will look back upon your life at the moments you spent with your loved ones. Invest in who's going to shed tears at your funeral. Think how sad it would be if no one mourned when you left this earth.

A few years ago, it was the day before Thanksgiving and I came across a picture that was taken at my last pro wrestling match in Orlando. It was the Pay Per View show, "Legends of Wrestling," and I was newly engaged to Darlene, my wonderful wife of today. The picture was of Darlene's sister Donna Mauro, and their beloved father, Charles Spezzi, holding a poster they made for the show. He passed away shortly after this day. Fortunately, I got to spend time with this amazing man and receive his blessing to marry his daughter.

My father-in-law Charles Spezzi and my sister-in-law Donna Mauro

Today, he is deeply missed, but he is never forgotten. The picture made me more aware than ever how important our time is with our friends and loved ones. Maybe that's why I'm up before 5:00 AM and stay up so late. I just don't want to miss a thing! I can't remember ever being so moved by the concept of Thanksgiving as I was that year, stumbling across that photo. I guess it's because I finally "got it." *When life gives you a hundred reasons to cry, God shows you a thousand reasons to smile.*

Maintain an attitude of gratitude.

Make it a habit to be thankful for the things and the people God places in your life. Happiness comes from spiritual wealth, not material wealth. For example, my wife doesn't care about expensive gifts or extravagant vacations. Although they may be nice, it's the little things that really matter to her — a love note, a kind word, spending time together, helping around the house. We count our blessings, not our money — and are grateful for each other.

My wife and I have another custom that keeps us focused on living each day like it's a gift, reminding us what's truly important. I've taken a large jar and filled it with marbles representing each Saturday left in

I'm losing my marbles!

my lifetime. Every weekend, Darlene and I walk out to our dock and say a prayer; we thank God for this beautiful life, our family, our marriage, our health — and reminisce about our week together. We then throw a marble into the lake. There is nothing like watching your time here on earth run out to help get your priorities straight.

To calculate how many Saturdays you have left, here's the formula: On average, people live about 75 years. If you multiply 75 times x 52 weeks in a year it equals 3,900 Saturdays in a lifetime. Let's say you're 40 years old. Take 75 minus 40 and that would leave 35 years. Take 35 years x 52 weeks = 1,820 Saturdays. Base on my age, I estimate that I only have 1,300 Saturdays left in my lifetime...

People get so fixated on making a living; they forget to make a life.

The "marble ritual" reminds us not to take our cherished moments for granted. I am much better now at remembering birthdays and anniversaries, and focusing in on the really important things. Realize how valuable life is... try the marble ritual. You don't have to have a lake. You can use woods or a field. Think of time as the currency of your life. It is the only "coin" you have, so spend it wisely.

There are no promises of tomorrow. Life passes quickly. There are no guarantees, no time outs, and often, no second chances, so don't let stress rob you of your precious time. Treasure every moment. Find something to smile about every day. Thank God throughout the day for his blessings and promises. Don't get caught in the trap of living for tomorrow; take time today for the people that you love.

The most beautiful things in life are most times the things you can't buy. Don't chase the

Realize what's really important!

35

money, find your passion. They say there is a pot of gold at the end of the rainbow. Be content with just the rainbow.

Appreciate the journey.

We are so often caught up in getting to our destination that we forget to enjoy the road we are on, especially the love and sacrifice of our family along the way. As I mentioned, my mother worked two jobs to make sure we had food on the table. She would do anything to try and make us happy, no matter how life's disappointments impacted her. Here's a great

> *"We make a living by what we get. We make a life by what we give."*
> WINSTON CHURCHILL

example. It was the Christmas of 1968. I was only eight years old. My sister Jodi was ten, and my brother Joel was six years old. We were so poor and had no money for presents, let alone a tree. It was the year that Dad left and my parents were divorced.

While I'm sure our mom was hurting on the inside just like us kids, she sat us down and told us there was no money for any gifts. We all understood and we all cried as a family. Not because of the lack of gifts, we all missed Dad.

Memorable Christmas

Early Christmas morning, Mom surprised us with the game *Hands Down*, by Ideal. Even

36

though she probably couldn't really afford the game, she knew it would give us a few hours of happiness. It turned out to be the most memorable Christmas ever because of the love we had for each other. The present was a nice surprise, but it was the gift of being together that was important.

As you give presents to those you love at Christmastime, or any time for that matter, keep in mind that the best gift you can give is the gift of yourself. The material things you give and receive each year are usually used up, broken and forgotten. But the gift of love and time with your loved ones will be forever cherished in everyone's hearts for eternity.

I've learned it's a lot more important to focus on the things we have than on the things we don't have. And if you are still having trouble appreciating the small things in life, take a lesson from a dog. We have three in our home — Kato, our German Shepherd, Maui, our Poodle/Maltese, and Rocco our little "morkie" (Maltese/Yorkshire Terrier mix). They are our resident entertainers. They are so fun, loyal, and lovable.

We learn a lot about happiness by observing our dogs. They live for love and give even more back. They appreciate the small things, a pat on the head, a scratch behind the ear, a little crumb dropped from the table. I look at Rocco and I think if he were a little smarter, he could tell me what he's thinking. Rocco looks at me as if saying, if you were a little smarter, I wouldn't have to!

Throughout my childhood and over the years I've always had a dog. And one of my saddest experiences was losing a dog. Dogs bring friendship and love into our lives — pure, unbridled joy. They teach us about trust. Nothing dims their foolish affection for us. I have become a better person by observing and seeking to understand canines. I've learned to live for today.

Going back to the little ditty that Clarice sang to Rudolph — while there isn't always tomorrow, there is one true part about the song: *Believe in your dreams come what may... with so much to do and so little time in a day.*

Live life to the fullest. Don't take your time on earth for granted. It's an extraordinary gift. Life is delicate and can disappear like a leaf in the wind. So tell someone what they mean to you; dance even if you don't know how; hold someone's hand, and appreciate every breath!

POZ Pointers

❖ Remind someone today how much you love them.
❖ Create a marble jar and cast one marble per week, proclaiming what was special.
❖ Write that long overdue "thank you" to someone who changed your life.

On the next page is the thank you note to my Boxing Coach and Mentor Ray Rinaldi:

Ray,

I have wanted to sit down and write you this letter for some time now. In church this week our Pastor talked about "If you only had one month to live, what would you do?" I wanted to make sure you knew how I felt and how grateful I am for all you have done and shown me. You have been such a big part of my life since I was 16 years old. You have been like a father to me, my coach, my good friend, my mentor. You have given me the greatest example of how to live a happy successful life. I have always said if there is one person I would like to be like it's you. You set the bar so high and I will spend the rest of my life trying to reach those incredible heights.

I think it is important that you know how much you helped this troubled kid. I know I went through some tough times in my life but it was your words that I always remembered when it was time to step up. No one has ever challenged me like you did. I am only one of thousands of kids that you made a difference in their lives. How many stores were not robbed, how many lives not taken, how many prison cells are empty because you showed compassion for so many of us kids. You have inspired people that are changing this world, giving back and making a difference. I will always represent the greatest man I have been blessed to know.

I love you with all my heart.

Marc Mero

Chapter Four: Make Someone's Day

Go ahead, make my day. By far, this is one of most famous catch-phrases in Hollywood history. Many of us can recall these words spoken by Clint Eastwood, playing the role of "Harry" in the 1983 film, *Sudden Impact.* For those of you too young to remember, Harry goes into a diner, discovers a robbery in progress, and guns down three of the robbers. As a surviving robber holds a fleeing waitress at gunpoint, threatening to shoot her, Harry — instead of backing off — points his .44 Magnum revolver into the man's face at point-blank range and dares him to shoot. Through clenched teeth and in the characteristic Eastwood grumble, he tempts: *"Go ahead, make my day."*

A grim illustration, yes, but a very important point. Making someone's day can be as straightforward as smiling, or as bold as risking your life for someone's, as did valiant Harry. Happiness comes from doing things for people that can make their day — and their life — better. Sometimes I imagine the people I meet have a big sign on their forehead that reads, "I want to feel special." So I do it — I make someone feel special. For it's not what we can get out of this life, it's what we do for others that truly matters.

There are two great commandments I stand by: Love God, and Love People. Every person we meet is an opportunity to be a source of energy and hope. One of the things Dr. Martin Luther King became famous for was giving a powerful speech about a dream of justice and freedom for everyone, what few people know is that he also prepared his own eulogy. He did not want to be remembered as a Nobel Peace Prize winner or for his many other awards. Instead, he wanted people to say "...that Martin Luther King, Jr., tried to love somebody." He wanted to be remembered for what he did for others.

Happiness is not expensive.

It's true that the best way to find happiness is by making others happy. Being the happiest person on the planet, I of course love to make people happy. Making someone's day does not require money or material rewards. Making someone happy takes little time and effort. It can be as easy as holding a door, saying "thank you," or "you're welcome." It can be as simple as a smile or a hug, or as inexpensive as a homemade card.

Bringing happiness to others can also involve being spontaneous or playful. And sometimes it's hard to tell who gets a bigger kick out of making someone's day, the giver or the receiver. For example, in a previous chapter, I mentioned "Matka," my mother-in-law. One of the things I like to do — believe it or not, it makes her smile — is to sneak up on her and her sister and try and scare them!

When we first started this silly game, my wife was afraid I might frighten them to death. That's a natural reaction I'll admit; after all, Matka is 87, and her sister Thecla, who also stays with us for months at a time, is 98. However, once my wife saw how much her own mother and aunt enjoyed this amusing activity, she began to indulge us. (I have the slight advantage — Matka is hearing impaired!) Nonetheless, being crept up on by her goofy son-in-law makes her day. We both find it funny. (And now so does my wife!)

Recently Matka was making chicken and broccoli for my lunch. She said, "Marc, I'm not sure if this broccoli is any good, can you smell it and let me know?" As I leaned over to smell the broccoli she pushed my head into the dish! I had broccoli all over my face. I still can't believe she did that! Who would have expected such a playful spirit in a woman her age? It brings me joy to know my antics contribute to her happiness.

Instead of complaining about life's little frustrations, try laughing about them.

Mother-in-law Gertie "Matka" Spezzi

Research has shown the health benefits of laughter range from strengthening the immune system to relieving stress. Often, the things that stress us out the most aren't nearly as bad as we initially think they are. How many times have you looked back and thought about how crazy you reacted to something pretty insignificant or worried over something that really wasn't that big of a deal?

I really believe that one of the reasons I am the self-proclaimed "happiest person on the planet" is because I love to laugh and to make others laugh. I laugh a lot with my wife and our family; we spend a lot of time sharing funny stories or acting silly. Try laughing and see how quickly a little fret can disappear. When was the last time you had a good laugh?

Happiness is flattering.

Making someone's day can be sharing a compliment or a few words of encouragement. *A word spoken at the right time is like golden apples on a silver tray.* Proverbs 25:11. Whether you realize it or not, there are so many people who need a hopeful word or a little bit of praise. Making others feel special entails seeing something unique in someone and pointing out what they might not have seen in themselves.

In my presentations I tell my audience, "You are amazing!" I'll say the same thing to you as my reader: *"You're marvelous!"* Now I know some of you are thinking he doesn't even know me. You're right, I may not know you, but

Aunt Thecla, 98 years young!

everyone has something wonderful about them. I see it all the time when I meet people. Maybe it's my positive outlook on life, but I do believe each of us is bestowed at least one special talent. I look for the good in everyone. We tend to be critical when we meet others, or focus on things about them we don't like. But when we start to believe there is something amazing about ourselves, then it becomes easier to find something amazing in every person we meet.

> *"Sometimes you put walls up not to keep people out, but to see who cares enough to break them down."*
> **UNKNOWN AUTHOR**

Happiness is miraculous.

Did you ever pray for something that you wanted so badly and you just couldn't understand why God didn't answer the way you wanted? It's happened to all of us who lift our petitions to a Holy God. But we only see life from our *limited* perspective. Here is my experience...

Guy, gone at 21 years old

Shortly after my mother passed, I was back on tour wrestling. I received a call that my younger brother Guy had a falling accident at the doctor's office. I thought to myself *how bad can you get hurt at a Doctor's office? Maybe he broke his arm or something?*

I was asked to get to the Sarasota hospital as soon as possible. I arrived at the hospital and rushed to the floor he was on. As I ran down the hall I could see family members and friends, many of whom were in tears. Guy had an unfortunate accident. He was only 21 years old and was on life-support. I remember the pain I saw on his beautiful wife Gina's face. She was eight months pregnant with their baby girl.

I was told my brother had gone to the doctor's office to get a drug test, required for a new job. Guy had always been afraid of having his blood taken; he would get nauseous or faint at the sight or thought of it. When the nurse opened the waiting room door and called his name, Guy stood up. But suddenly he fell back and hit his head hard on the floor... Guy's anxiety to needles caused him to pass out.

When I arrived at the hospital room and discovered the severity of his injury, I asked everyone to please leave his room. I wanted to be alone with my little brother. I got down on my knees, reached through the rails of his hospital bed, held his hand and prayed for a miracle.

I said, "God, I don't ask for much; I really need a miracle. Please don't take him... he's only 21... he just got married... he's going to be a daddy. You just took my mother two weeks ago. I begged God... please, please don't take him!"

Praying for a miracle...

The doctor came in the room and placed his hand on my shoulder. As I looked up he said, "I'm sorry, there's no brain activity." I said, "No!... God's going to give us a miracle." He looked in my eyes and said, "I'm so sorry."

Good-bye Guy.

At the time it was really hard to understand why my desperate plea and the prayers of my family were not answered. But God *took* Guy because it was his *time*. When Guy died, we donated his heart and other vital organs. This compassionate act of generosity saved the lives of five other people. From Heaven, my brother was able to "make the day" for those five individuals, and their families and friends. A month later his precious baby daughter Vollica, our beautiful niece, was born.

God did give many miracles, just not ours, or in the manner we hoped. But new miracles have risen as God continues to use Guy's life and death in unexpected ways.

45

The gift of life, Vollica

I speak about my little brother in all my presentations, and his story has made so many people aware of just how precious life is. It has brought families together and made people more sensitive to their choices. It has broken down barriers and bridged the gap in many relationships — establishing greater bonds of love.

There is no greater joy than knowing you helped changed someone's life — and God turned a tragedy into triumph by illustrating this principle through Guy. I can look back with more love than I have ever known for a little brother that I miss so much!

Happiness is contagious.

I can only think of one thing greater than being happy and that is to help another person be happy too. I find that when I smile long enough, most people smile back. Since I started doing for others, I have been flooded with happiness. I have attracted the most fascinating people I could have ever imagined meeting. God brings people in your life and they just seem to show up at the right time.

No matter how good or bad your day has gone, let those you live with count on a big smile from you when you walk in the door. Let them see that JOY in you. Even if you have a big family, focus on one person at a time, giving your undivided attention. Connect with family members, your roommate, or your dog, cat or iguana — and then do something positive for them. All it takes is letting others know you are thinking about them and that you care.

Listening is a simple way to make someone's day. In fact, research has found that remarkable things can happen if parents and caregivers spend at least 15 minutes of undivided time a day listening and talking with their children. Just these few minutes a day can be instrumental in building a healthier and safer future.

Listening is a powerful way to say, "I care." Some would argue that men need to learn this lesson the most. I know I did! I never realized how much improvement I needed in this area until I found myself alone, without companionship. When I met my wife Darlene, I was determined not to make the same mistake again!

Poor listening skills become a habit if we don't catch it and correct it early on. If you have ever been told you don't listen well enough, be more patient and stop thinking of what you are going to say next. Really listen… and let the other person express themselves and finish without interruption. If, on the other hand, people tell you that you *are* a good listener, you have a valuable gift.

It's time we all start showing compassion for others. We *all* need to use our unique talents to create hope and inspire each other. Show compassion. Give to others for no other reason than to make them happy. Reach out and touch someone. As I've stressed in an earlier chapter, one of the greatest gifts you can give is the gift of attention. Give of yourself, your time, your heart, and your abundance, to someone that needs help. The more you give, the more you get back. Giving while you're living — so you're knowing where it's going — brings joy to your heart and others!

Smile more, play more, and say kind and caring things. At the end of the day, the happiest person on the planet will be you!

POZ Pointers:

❖ Share a laugh.
❖ Give a compliment.
❖ Listen… really listen, until your ears burn.
❖ Remember someone's birthday, anniversary, or other special occasion.

Chapter Five: Surround yourself with POZ people

*F*riends are like elevators. They either take you up, or they take you down.

The last chapter was about making someone's day and the importance of being a positive power in someone's life, by listening, smiling, or sharing a kind word. Equally important is making sure you surround yourself with the same kind of positive energy. Take a look around you. There are great people, some real champions who can inspire you and lift you up. They are rooting for you. But unfortunately, there are also some real losers, people who want to drag you down. They are rooting against you. So what will the verdict be? The outcomes are your choice. Who do you choose to hang with?

It seems like every year a film comes out portraying the consequences of getting mixed up in the wrong crowd. The

> *"Keep away from those who try to belittle your ambitions. Small people always do that, but the really great make you believe that you too can become great."*
> MARK TWAIN

1995 *The Basketball Diaries* is about "Jim" and his Catholic school chums who all play for the best basketball team in New York. But then a dying friend, an immoral coach, and other teenage shenanigans cause them to get kicked off the team after being caught using drugs. For Jim, hanging with the wrong crowd spirals downward as he turns to the streets, betrays friends, robs stores, and deals drugs to feed his heroin addiction. All of these bad choices ruin his dream of becoming a basketball star.

The list of wayward-friend illustrations goes back to Hollywood history, and sadly, they reflect "real" situations in our lives today. One of the most important lessons I have learned almost at every turn is how important it is to surround yourself with positive people.

Today, I invest in relationships that are encouraging and rewarding. I choose to spend time with optimistic people who are supportive such as my family, mentors, and close friends. These are the individuals who are honest, appreciative, and kind. In other words, I surround myself with other "champions of choices" — people who say and do the right things.

But it wasn't always this way. In my earlier years I got involved with friends who influenced me to drink, smoke, and do drugs. They may have influenced me, but ultimately it was my choice. I recall the circumstance in my life that set me on a path to destruction.

It was just two weeks before my first pro boxing match, and I had my nose shattered in an accident. After reconstruction surgery I was told by my Doctor it would be about a year before I could go back to full contact in boxing. So I wasn't able to make the fight, nor do any sports for that matter. I was disappointed about missing my pro debut, and my mother, my greatest supporter, encouraged me as they were about to wheel me down the hall to surgery: "Don't worry, Son, you'll be back in a year and you'll be champ of the world!"

Without something to train for, I suddenly found myself with extra time on my hands. In other words, I wasn't preparing for a football game, hockey game or boxing match. I agreed to join my friends at a party. We were down in a basement, where a couple of guys had gone out for a "beer run." They started passing out cans of beer, and they offered me one. My friend sitting next to me held up his beer and said "Cheers."

Right then and there, I had a choice. Ironically, my first thought was of my mother — not about how bad she would punish me — but how my "choice" would break her heart. She had worked her whole life to take care of us and taught us about making the right choices. But that night, I was with the "cool kids" — or at least I thought they were. "Cheers"... I drank it.

Week after week I did this, and before I knew it, alcohol led to other drugs. *Don't worry*, I thought to myself and said to others, "I'll be back in one year and be champ of the world!" One year became two years; two years became four years; and four years became ten years. I threw away ten years of my life, making bad choices. The only job I could get without a good education was digging swimming pools.

Digging for a living

When I was a child, I'd written down in my little book I wanted to have a Cadillac and a big house, and be a millionaire. I wanted to be somebody! Instead I found myself in a place I never imagined — at the bottom of a swimming pool, digging for a living. I remember saying to myself, *I don't belong here*. I had expected more out of myself and life. Did you ever feel like that?

Show me your friends and I'll show you your future.

It wasn't until ten years later that I got a second chance. I sat in my living room with some friends and we were channel surfing. Pro Wrestling appeared on the TV screen and I shouted: "Stop it there, let me watch this. I can do that!"

It was that "Ah-ha" moment. My friends thought I was crazy. They said, "Marc, those guys are so big; they will pick you up and throw you out of the ring. You're 30 years old, you don't have a chance."

I was convinced I could become a wrestler! I took action toward a new goal in my life. I found out where a wrestling school was located and drove an hour every weekend to pursue my new goal. One year later I signed a big contract with World Championship Wrestling (WCW). While I became successful at pro wrestling and went on to become "rich and famous," something was still missing.

On the road, I hung around with celebrities, but many of them were negative influences and so I resumed my bad habits of partying and doing drugs. I remember one wrestling match in particular when I was in WCW. Backstage with some of the other wrestlers after a match, I was given a drug (to this day I still am not sure what it was). When I took it, I immediately felt sick. I knew something was very wrong as I felt myself losing consciousness. I was carried to a car and left in the backseat with the hopes I'd be "okay later." No one called for help.

Another time I was in Florida with "friends" and we were getting high smoking cocaine. The last thing I remember was smoking the pipe and then waking up the next day with all my friends standing around me. Some were near tears because they thought I was going to die. Again, no one had called for help. I was fortunate to be alive! But even near death experiences didn't keep me from continuing my destructive lifestyle.

When all these bad choices started catching up with me — coupled with the devastating loss of numerous friends and several family members in a shockingly short period — I got down on my knees and asked God to help me. I asked Him to come into my life and change me. Before this, it was me always trying to change someone else.

My sister Jodi

Now, fast forward eight years later. My life is now amazing! I am married to the woman I believe God intended me to be with; I have the greatest relationship with my sister Jodi and brother Joel. We have all found our passion in life! Jodi owns and runs an animal rescue in Kirkville, New York. Ironically, Joel owns a large pool company in Alpharetta, Georgia. (I hope I never have to ask him for a job!)

I'm blessed by friends who are a positive influence in my life. I am committed to working on and

My brother Joel

53

strengthening relationships. I surround myself with people that inspire me to dream bigger than I ever imagined possible.

Purge the negative influences in your life.

Here is one action step I have personally taken that has kept me on a positive path. Each January when the New Year rolls around, I scroll through all the numbers I've collected in my cell phone over that past year, and contemplate each name. If an individual is not a positive influence in my life, they get deleted from my phone. Gone in a click! Don't let anyone steal your joy or lead you down a path of negativity.

When you choose your friends, choose them well. For a positive relationship to grow, remember what is important — someone who can be trusted and someone whose shoulder you can lean on. A positive person will speak with wisdom and encourage you to do the right thing. A good friend leads you down the right road. A loyal friend believes in your dreams.

Always be careful about who you share your dreams and goals with. Sadly many people, and even family members, will tell you why you can't do something. They tell you why something costs too much, or why you'll never make it happen... why you're not big enough or fast enough or smart enough.

Sometimes, the reason people tell you why you can't do something is because they can't do it! They may not want you to be happy or successful if they can't be. These people aren't your friends.

But sometimes good-meaning friends or family may discourage you from accomplishing a dream or goal because they want to "protect" you.

A true friend or partner is someone who understands you, who listens and supports you when you are struggling, forgives you when you fail, celebrates your successes with you, and most importantly, believes in you.

Sometimes the decision to sever an unhealthy relationship can seem like the hardest thing in the world to do. People can be addicted to a person, just like they can be addicted or controlled by drugs and alcohol. Are you struggling with this issue? It may take all the prayer and power you can muster, but is one of the most important choices you must make. Trust God… leave abusive relationships. Get the help you need from a pastor, school counselor, or friend. **Don't put a question mark where God puts a period!**

Making right choices opens the door to God's best for you.

After failed relationships, my heart was broken and hardened. I wondered if I could ever learn to trust again… to open my heart to new relationships. But when I finally did, I received the best reward life could offer. I married Darlene — my best friend! There is no feeling more beautiful than knowing you are right next to the one you love.

Once I took steps to get my life healthy, balanced and whole — by making right choices — I was ready to receive the blessings and gifts God wanted to give me. I became a POZ person and that attracted other positive people into my life. God puts people in our lives to teach us, and I am learning much.

The most precious possession I ever have been blessed with is my wife's heart. When you love deeply you never grow old; I may die of old age, but my heart will die young. Quoting the wise cartoon character, Winnie the Pooh, "If you live to be 100, I hope I live to be 100 minus one day, so I never have to live without you."

Ask God to guide you in your relationship choices. Then, love without fear. Love is worth fighting for, being brave for, risking everything for. Once your heart is in the right place, be willing to go out on a limb and love someone unselfishly. Be willing to protect that relationship, guard it and cherish it with all you have!

One of the ways I express my love to Darlene is by being a "candle of light" in her world. There is nothing that touches my heart or makes me happier than seeing Darlene's face light up. My love toward her radiates, and is reflected back to me. I love being married and I love being in love. At the end of the day, I can't wait to get home to my Pumpkin! Are people happy to see you?

The Love of my Life

No matter how challenging a day I had, or how rough Darlene's day may have been, because I have chosen to be a positive person she can always count on seeing me with an enormous smile and outstretched arms. When I plant a big kiss on her face, she feels my joy and energy. Let people experience the positive joy that is in you. As you make a choice to cultivate and share "positivity" with others, you will begin to find yourself surrounded by more and more POZ people. It is a great place to be!

Speak positive blessings into the lives of others.

There is an old saying: sticks and stones will break my bones but words will never hurt me. That is the biggest lie ever! I've met plenty of kids who would rather be beat up than be called a name. The greatest damage we do to each other is

> *"Love is always the answer to healing of any sort. And the pathway to love is forgiveness."*
> **LOUISE HAY**

through angry or mean spirited words. What makes matters worse is that we tend to forget this when it comes to the people that mean the most to us.

Remember how I treated my mom? "I just want to be left alone!" And my little brother? "Go away, you little punk!" Cruel words can hurt more than any physical assault, and the resulting wounds may take even longer to heal. Just like the biggest forest fires are started by the smallest spark, the tongue is one of the smallest parts of the body, but it can do some of the worst damage.

I remember in sixth grade when another student made fun of the way I looked. I still recall that horrible feeling whenever I think back on those days. It was in study hall, and a student said out loud that I looked like a bum. My mother would buy our clothes at garage sales, and I was always embarrassed that we could never afford nicer things. I can still feel the humiliation from having second-hand clothing. In fact, one time, I had a classmate say to me, "I used to have a t-shirt just like that, except mine had a red stain under the arm." I lifted my arm, and there was the red stain. When I realized my mom bought the t-shirt at his parent's garage sale, I felt my face go flush.

I know I'm not alone in this feeling of despair. Every week I receive letters and e-mails from students; most of them are so positive and beautiful to read. But some of them are from young people who are victims of bullying, scorned by their parents or peers, or lonely and depressed because they are shunned by others just because they are different.

For example, I often read letters from students who are ridiculed due to problems with their weight. My heart goes out to these kids because I understand and feel their pain. At

> *"Anyone who claims to live in God's light and hates a brother or sister is still in the dark."*
> **LOUISE HAY**

Champion of Choices we recently started our **Family Obesity Initiative** to help families deal with obesity-related illnesses and social issues surrounding self-esteem and self confidence.

It is heartbreaking when others are relentlessly bullied — and the consequences can be tragic. I read about a beautiful student named Kristina Calico who wrote this poem in her journal:

> *I knew I was the ugly one, don't say that's a lie because you don't know what kids have said and done. It hurts to think about how mean some people could be. Even when I started to look a little better, they still couldn't see. The only reason I even bother to tell you my sad sob story is that someday the public might know what a teenage girl goes through. So as you know nice guys finish last, well it might as well be nice girls finish last, too.*

Kristina took her life.

I received another letter not too long ago from a young girl in high school who was the subject of much verbal abuse at school, and she wrote, "I just want to tell you thank you for coming to my high school because that day I saw you, I was planning to kill myself and then you told me about your life and what you went through. I want to live."

Emily, another 17-year-old student in New York, has been having suicidal thoughts for over a year now. She wrote to me that she'd started hanging around with the wrong kind of kids at school who talked her into doing drugs, and this choice had caused her to alienate her family. Now she is working on turning her life around, dealing with the scorn from others.

Dominic, another teenager, wrote to tell me he hopes that after students hear me speak at his school, he will not be bullied anymore.

By definition, bullying is more than just name calling. It's pushing, tripping, incessant teasing, belittling, excluding, playing repeated dirty tricks, and spreading rumors. Every day in our communities, people are teased, threatened, or tormented by others. Bullying has drawn growing concern from parents, educators, and lawmakers everywhere. It's a problem that creates an environment of fear, oppression, and violence.

There are innumerable sad stories of students threatening, wounding, and even killing each other every year. Case studies of the shooting at Columbine High School and other U.S. schools have suggested that bullying was a factor in many of the incidents. In 1997, Reena Virk was murdered by school mates in Canada. In 1999, two boys who were bullied by classmates, walked into their high school in Littleton, Colorado, with guns and bombs and killed 12 students, a teacher, and injured 18 others. They then turned the guns on themselves.

And there are an even greater number of suicides that have resulted from bullying referred to as "bullicide." Consider for example, Phoebe

Make a difference in someone's life

Prince, the freshman at South Hadley High School who decided to hang herself in early 2010 due to constant taunting. Classmates were charged with multiple felon indictments.

Bullying is a problem that affects people of ALL ages, but especially young people.

Statistics on the rates of bullying and cyber bullying (through Facebook and text messaging) vary based on questions asked and populations studied. The general consensus is that one out of three children is bullied at school, in neighborhoods, or online.

Here are just a few staggering facts reported according to the Bureau of Justice School Crime and Safety:

➤ Each day 160,000 students miss school for fear of being bullied.
➤ 87% say shootings are motivated by a desire to "get back at those who have hurt them."
➤ 28% of youths who carry weapons have witnessed violence at home.
➤ 100,000 students carry a gun to school.

This past year I had the honor to speak at the 11th annual "Kicks for Guns" program founded by Orlando radio personality and great friend Russ Rollins.

Russ Rollins and his incredible team,
Monsters of the Morning Radio Show

This program encourages people to give up their guns, "no questions asked," in exchange for sneakers. Because of the efforts of Russ Rollins and his incredible morning-show team, Monsters of the Morning, thousands of guns have been taken off our streets and no doubt countless lives saved.

How do you treat or influence others? Using the elevator analogy I spoke of earlier: Do you take them up, or do you take them down? We have an impact on other people's lives.

The greatest commandment is to love God; the next is to love people. We must not belittle each other, and we shouldn't let others demean us. Stand up for yourself, get help, or find a new set of surroundings. When we are insulted, our personal sense of value is attacked. We are left feeling unloved, unsafe, and worthless. Words can inflict wounds that last a lifetime.

Be a positive influence, and surround yourself with positive people. Stay away from negative pressures, negative people, and negative persuasions. It's a choice that only you can make.

POZ Pointers

❖ Erase all the numbers in your phone of people who don't bring a positive influence to your life.
❖ Chose your words wisely, they can scar people forever or bless them beyond measure.
❖ Just say "No" to bad choices.

If you or someone you know suffers from the cruelty of bullying, or any kind of mistreatment, please reach out to someone you trust for help, or call the

Suicide Crisis Hotline
800-273-TALK
800-273-8255
Toll-Free 24 Hours, 7 Days a Week

Chapter Six: Let it go.

Forgive and forget.

$\mathcal{E}$asier said than done, right? We've all heard the truism: "To forget is human, to forgive is divine."

In the last chapter, we looked at what it feels like to be ridiculed. Now it's time to look at the toughest part of dealing with people who hurt you. Forgiving them. Harder than tolerating mockery, more difficult than dealing with scorn, more complicated than bearing the pain of emotional abuse is finding the power and will to forgive.

The 1989 animated Disney film based on the Hans Christian Andersen fairy tale of Ariel is about a young mermaid princess who is dissatisfied with life under the sea and curious about the human world. Ignoring her father's wishes, Ariel often goes to the ocean's surface to explore this off-limits domain.

Eventually, Ariel falls in love with a human, Prince Eric, whom she saves from drowning. Her father, King Triton, notices a change in Ariel's demeanor, furiously confronts her, and destroys her human treasures. But later out of love, the King sends help for his daughter who is caught up in the evil powers of the sea-witch Ursula. He also forgives her for betraying him and breaks the evil spell. After seeing that Ariel really loves Eric, he willingly changes her from a mermaid into a human.

Even though it's just a fairytale, it also illustrates the value of forgiving someone when they have made a choice that hurts us. This story is a classic, and we call them classics for a reason — the message is timeless. We've all been injured by the actions or words of another. Perhaps a parent or sibling criticizes us, a peer makes fun of us, or maybe our partner or best friend betrays us. These wounds can leave lasting feelings of anger and bitterness, and may even conjure up feelings of vengeance. But if we don't learn to forgive, we may be the one who pays.

He who angers you controls you.

When we're hurt by someone we love and trust, we become angry, sad or confused. Dwelling on these negative feelings, we may find ourselves drowning in self pity or consumed by bitterness or a sense of unfairness. While it may seem virtually impossible to absolve someone who has done us wrong, life is just too short to waste harboring resentment or wishing harm on someone. In fact, the best revenge against someone who you feel wronged by is forgiveness.

When we are wronged, we have a choice to either forgive or relive. Reliving past grievances only gets in the way of the joy and happiness that is meant for us. Holding a grudge jeopardizes your own well-being. It eats away at you and leaves you feeling broken. Lack of forgiveness creates anger and bitterness, and these harbored emotions are toxic.

Whether we are conscious of it or not, these underlying emotions affect our day-to-day experiences and our interactions with others. When we are stuck in a place of un-forgiveness we lose sight of our joy, passion, and aspirations. Our life becomes so obsessed by past wrong-doings that we aren't able to focus on the present, and we lose sight of our dreams for the future.

Forgiveness doesn't mean accepting the pain or approving someone's bad will. You aren't expected to deny a person's responsibility for hurting you. You can forgive someone without excusing the act. I've learned that when I make a decision with an open heart I usually make the right decision. You have to learn to forgive.

65

When someone has hurt you, it's an opportunity to change your attitude to include thoughts of love, understanding, and harmony, regardless of what the other person has done.

Forgive or Re-live

Forgiveness is about setting *yourself* free, more than setting the other person free.

Holding in bitterness, resentment or not forgiving others hurts you! The person who offended you may not realize the full effect of their actions, or give their behavior a second thought. Dwelling on the grievance wastes your mental energy, and accomplishes nothing. Good communication, on the other hand, plays an important role. Approaching people in a calm and loving manner can often mend the hurt or prevent it from intensifying.

While forgiveness does not change the past, it does enlarge the future. The action or words that hurt you may always remain a part of your life, but practicing forgiveness can weaken the grip on you and help you focus on the positive parts of your life. You can't have a better tomorrow if you are thinking about yesterday all the time. As you let go of grudges and make room in your heart for forgiveness, you'll no longer define your life by your wounds. You may even find compassion and understanding.

Seek the strength to rid your mind of thoughts like *How could they?* Or *Why did they?* Learn to focus less on the pain another person caused, and more on what you can do to get past it. When people let you down, try to think of positive things about them — what they once did to help you, support you, or make you smile.

Did this person teach you something? Maybe through the experience, you've gained a new perspective on how to treat others better — or how *not* to treat them. Also, sometimes people take the wrong road before they find the one that they are supposed to be on. You could be the person who helps them get back on track. Tell them, "If you could see only half of what I see in you, then one day you'll realize how truly amazing you are." Boldly take the first step to restore the relationship.

So how do you get to this state of forgiveness? Like attitude, or "Thinking POZ," a state of forgiveness is a choice. We are so quick to anger and quick to blame, but so slow to forgive and even slower to forget. Begin by shifting your energies from judgment to joy.

Steps for Letting Go

1. Reflect on how the negative situation impacted you.
2. Consider how you've reacted and dealt with it.
3. Think about how these feelings and actions have affected your well-being.
4. Summon the grace and strength to forgive.

So how do you know when you're finally over someone or something? When have you truly forgiven? First off, when someone mentions the name or the event and you don't get angry anymore! But mainly, you'll know when you've forgiven someone because feelings of harmony replace feelings of hostility. Peace replaces pain. This is when you have forgiven someone.

One of the reasons I am now the "happiest person on the planet" is because of forgiveness. I remember when my former wife of almost ten years decided she had enough, and wanted a divorce. I was angry, I was hurt; I went through a gamut of emotions. I had already lost my family — and now my wife. I felt vindictive, spiteful. I was geared up to fight over every possession we had acquired.

Yet by the time we had to face a judge and finalize our divorce, we walked into the courtroom, hand in hand. We ended up splitting everything. And, after we signed the divorce papers, we hugged good-bye and wished each other well. From that day onward, I hoped the best for her and I never spoke a bad word about her.

Surrendering the hurt can help you gain a peace that surpasses understanding.

How did it all change? I asked God to help me forgive, and I came to realize that bitterness and "getting even" was not healthy or productive. Now, as I look back, I know that door of resentment would have had to eventually close for me to notice the door of happiness that stood open before me — my wife Darlene. I never thought this level of happiness existed. Forgiveness leads to amazing results!

Here's what else I've noticed… Forgiveness brings a kind of peace that helps you go on with life. "Peace" is not a physical absence of noise, woes, or daily responsibilities. To be at peace means to be in the midst of those daily challenges and still have calmness in your heart. Peace is something you seek, pray for, receive and then give away. If you are at odds with someone, you are not at peace. Through forgiveness, I am at peace with myself. What does your "peace meter" register?

God has a purpose for all our lives. When I allow God to work through me, to do HIS will, I feel at peace. I have no animosity toward others. I love doing for others… helping, guiding, sharing, and being there when people really need me — being that person God intended.

While forgiveness may not always be easy, it is always worth it.

Forgiveness is essential for happiness. We have to accept the past and trust God with our future. Among situations that we experience and witness throughout our lives, some will be easier to forgive than others. However, I'm willing to go out on a limb and say that forgiveness is possible in all situations. I have no bitterness and hold no anger. And I have watched my life change because I have accepted my past and forgiven everyone and everything.

I have realized there are no rewards for past regrets. Yesterday is the tomb, today is the womb! Today is a great day to move on, a great day to make peace with your past. Choose to forgive yourself and others, just as God has forgiven us. Ask God for help with this life-changing choice — and you, too, can be the happiest person on the planet!

POZ Pointers

❖ Don't get even, be even tempered. Your reaction is a choice.

❖ Let go of baggage. On little strips of paper, write down situations you are bitter about. Now crumple them up and put them in a brown paper bag. Next, wad up your "Bitter Bag" and throw it away! Two points if you make the shot from across the room!

❖ Tell someone who wronged you that they are forgiven.

Chapter Seven: Do the right thing.

One of life's greatest gifts is free will. Choice! You have the ability to choose one course of action over another to achieve a goal, or to do the right thing.

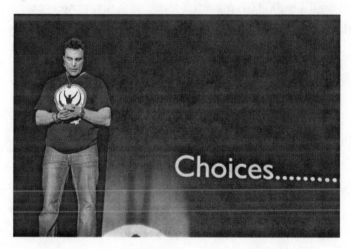

We make choices every day, and our lives become fuller, richer — or more complicated because of them. We decide where to buy our food, how to spend our time, and whether or not to take action toward our dreams. We decide who our friends are. We decide how to treat others. Because every choice we make leads us closer to or further from our goals, we need to constantly examine where we are on our journey.

We are defined by our choices.

Whenever I am at a crossroads I always ask myself, *am I doing the right thing?* It's a small question that leads to titanic consequences, so we have to figure out what really is the right thing.

Do the Right Thing is actually the title of a 1989 movie directed by Spike Lee, who also starred in the film as Mookie, a young black man working at a pizzeria in multi-ethnic community. "Sal," the pizzeria's owner, is harassed by the neighbors to place pictures of black celebrities on the restaurant's "Wall of Fame." Sal argues it's his business; he's proud of his Italian heritage, and he doesn't have to feature anyone but Italians on his wall. This prompts some vandalism and eventual violent behavior when, one night, a large crowd threatens hostility against Sal and his family.

In the nick of time, Mookie chooses to "do the right thing." He throws a trash can through the window of Sal's restaurant, directing the collective anger toward the property and away from the owners. Although the restaurant burns to the ground, their lives are spared and the film ends with two quotations presenting opposing choices. The first is from Dr. Martin Luther King, Jr. that argues that violence is never justified under any circumstances. The second, from Malcolm X, argues that violence is not violence, but "intelligence" when it is self-defense. *Which one is the "right" choice?*

> *"Have the courage to say no. Have the courage to face the truth. Do the right thing because it is right. These are the magic keys to living your life with integrity."*
> W. CLEMENT STONE

Doing the right thing is sometimes more difficult than it may seem. There are going to be shades of grey, and when this happens, we sometimes deceive ourselves. We justify our actions or make excuses for not doing what we need or should do.

The real challenge is that whenever we are at a fork in the road, the easiest path isn't necessarily the best one to take. When we act out of habit or instinct rather than conscious choice, the road before us can be a slippery slope.

Have you ever found yourself saying, "why did I just do that?" or "what made me do that?" When we choose to act contrary to our beliefs, often it's too late and the damage is done. My dad used to say: **"When bad things happen they always started out as a good idea."**

Reputations are built over a lifetime, but they can be destroyed in the blink of an eye. One way to avoid compromising your morals is to decide what you want to be known for, and how you want to be remembered. Then make sure your actions line up with your values and beliefs. In other words, your "walk" should match your "talk."

The road to good choices is led by your conscience.

The good news is we have an "internal compass" to help us navigate. Instead of being impulsive, stop and evaluate the "truth" of a situation. Be honest with yourself — your future and very life may depend upon the choices you make in the heat of the moment. And no question, doing the right thing takes strength and courage. Sometimes, you have to take a stand against what might be the more popular route. You might have to say "no" when everyone else is saying "yes." You might have to bravely defend your own or someone else's honor. Chances are when something feels wrong it probably is wrong.

Remember the chapter about those who bully and demean others? The right thing to do is to stand up to the enemy, and this takes guts. As you gain confidence and build discipline, you will find that, over time, making the distinction between right and "not right" — and doing something about it — becomes easier.

Since I rededicated my life to Christ, I have experienced "peace of mind" and the positive effects that come from making the best choices.

Peace and successes are not about luck or fate; but rather, the natural blessings that result from doing the right things.

If you aren't sure what path to take, start by using your good, God-given sense. Sometimes it's just a matter of choosing between what's good for you and what isn't. For example, that time when my friends offered me a beer in the basement, it wasn't just a moral choice. It wasn't just about what my mother would think. Drinking — in excess — just isn't good for you. It can lead to bad health or danger when making choices. Learn how to decide what is best for you all the way around. **As the saying goes, if you don't stand for something, you'll fall for anything.**

Once you know what course you're supposed to be on, pay attention each day to your routine and decide if each action is really the best way to go. Ask yourself at every turn, *am I doing the right thing? Does this uphold my values? Does this support my dreams?* Anything that pulls your focus away from your priorities is bound to distract you from your life purpose and slow you down from what's truly important. At each juncture along the path of destiny, we need to ask ourselves, *am I moving closer to my goals? Do my actions align with what I believe?*

And when we realize we aren't on the right path, we need to take corrective action. We must realign ourselves with our goals and our values. Coming from a sports' background, I sometimes think of life as a sport. It's about making the best plays (choices). It's about playing by the rules. It's also about looking out for your teammates.

Steer clear of paths to "nowhere."

Finally, beware of paths to nowhere — namely the road of inaction. Laziness or idleness has consequences. As Shakespeare

> *"Nobody ever drowned in their own sweat."*
> ANN LANDERS

once said, "if you choose not to decide, you still have made a choice." Refusal to act is a choice. The refusal is our decision. And by refusing, we turn over our destiny to chance. Instead of taking charge, we drift or we leave ourselves open to temptation.

While free-will is a great gift, it doesn't come without a price. The price is responsibility. When we think about our responsibilities as burdens we *have to do*, the result is dread and stress. But when we accept and carry out our responsibility — and think of our duties, school and our jobs as things we *get to do* — the reward is happiness and a fulfilled life.

Don't worry, be happy!

Keep in mind that regrets and worries are two things that can ruin your life. *Some regrets are not about what we did, but rather what we didn't do.* Be willing to forgive yourself, whether you make a mistake of "omission" or "commission." And, when it comes to worrying, don't do it. According to research

> ➤ 40% of our worries never happen
> ➤ 32% of our worries concern the past
> ➤ 16% of our worries are needless concerns
> ➤ 12% of our worries are insignificant and petty issues.

So, as you can see, worrying about the past, holding on to regrets, or stressing over things you can't control is a fruitless pursuit. Part of doing the right thing is coming to terms with the fact that you're not perfect, and that you will make mistakes. God loves you anyway. Turn your worries, regrets and cares over to Him… He's up all night!

POZ Pointers

❖ Today, make up your mind to break one bad habit. Use prayer, perseverance and the support of friends and family to help you get on track, and stay there.

❖ Ask yourself at every turn, "am I doing the right thing?"

❖ The next time you make a decision, ask yourself "is this in line with what I believe… what I want out of life?"

❖ Don't worry about things you can't control.

Chapter Eight: Get back up.

It's not about how many times you get knocked down; it's how many times you get back up.

$\mathcal{D}$o you ever feel like you've been knocked down one too many times? If you haven't seen the 1976 sports drama *Rocky*, starring Sylvester Stallone, you've probably heard of the legendary Rocky Balboa. Rocky starts out as a club fighter who gets a shot at the world heavyweight championship.

Although Rocky trains hard, as the underdog he doesn't really expect to win; he just wants to go the distance with his opponent, "Apollo Creed," which no fighter has ever done. The fight indeed goes 15 rounds, with each fighter suffering many injuries. In the end, even though Creed is declared the winner, the competitive spirit of the formerly unknown fighter who "gets back up" several times gives the film a classic appeal that made it a surprise hit — the highest grossing film that year and the winner of three Oscars, including Best Picture.

Now come on, admit it! Have you caught yourself gingerly humming the theme song "Gonna Fly Now" whenever the going gets tough? No doubt, "Rocky" is a household name, associated with toughness and determination. As a matter of fact, I even named our puppy "Rocco!"

Our mixed-breed terrier came from my sister Jodi who adopted him through her Kirkville Animal Rescue and Education center in Kirkville, New York. He's a scrawny little thing. But from the beginning Rocco was such a valiant fighter. He has become an amazing new family

Rocco "The Wonder Dog" Mero

member who entertains and inspires many. He even has his own Facebook page: Rocco "The Wonder Dog" Mero!

There are plenty of "real-life" heroes who have demonstrated this kind of determination. Michael Jordan was arguably one of the best basketball players of all time, and he attributes his successes to his failures. He never gave up; even he said, "I've missed more than 9,000 shots in my career. I've lost almost 300 games. Twenty-six times I've been trusted to take the game-winning shot and missed. I've failed over and over and over again in my life. And that is why I succeed."

> *"Only those who dare to fail greatly can achieve greatly."*
> JOHN F. KENNEDY

And of course there was champion cyclist Lance Armstrong, diagnosed with serious cancer; yet, despite the odds, he overcame the threats to his health and set out to win the Tour de France six years in a row.

One of my favorite inspirational athletes is Derek Redmond, a 1992 contender for the 400 event in the summer Olympics. I like to tell his story in my presentations. While he may not have taken home a medal, he defines the essence of the human spirit. Because of an Achilles tendon injury, he was forced to withdraw from the 400 at the 1988 Games, only ten minutes before the race. He then underwent five surgeries over the next year. But when the 1992 Games came around, Redmond was "back up" so to speak. It was to be his comeback — his moment to show the world what he was made of. And that's exactly what he did.

The stadium was packed with 65,000 fans, and the race began with Redmond breaking out in from the rest and quickly taking the lead. But on the backstretch, only 175 meters away from finishing, Redmond pulled his right hamstring. He started hopping, but then fell. Laying on the track, he told the medical crew, "There's no way I'm getting on that stretcher. I'm going to finish my race."

In a moment that will live forever in the minds of millions, Redmond struggled to his feet and through tears, disappointment and anguish he started hobbling down the track. The other runners had finished, with Steve Lewis of the U.S. taking the race. Yet with great perseverance, one painful step at a time — and with the support of his father who had made his way through the crowd to the track — Redmond limped onward toward the finish line. Now that's determination!

Life isn't always about winning the race; life is about finishing the race.

Biblical wisdom on this topic is found in Hebrews 12:1 where we read: *...let us run with perseverance the race that is marked out for us.* Likely, most of you have never competed in an Olympic marathon or stepped inside a boxing ring. But because you are a contender in the "Game of Life" you experience setbacks, disappointment, and heartache. We all do. Maybe you've lost a job, flunked a test, or failed to make the sports team or cheerleading squad. Maybe you've had to say good-bye to loved ones way sooner than you ever imagined. Maybe there are days you feel that if one more "bad thing" happens, you just can't face it. I can honestly say I have felt that way.

Some circumstances can be especially difficult. When friends or loved-ones pass on, or when our dreams appear to vanish into thin air — it hurts! The pain may last an hour, or a day, or a year; yet eventually the scars will heal. But if you give up, that pain can last forever.

In fact, I once believed my happiest days were behind me. I wasn't sure I could ever heal from my losses. I wasn't following my dream. I wasn't doing the right thing. In trying to "Keep up with the Joneses," I had lost my way. I was caught up in a selfish cycle where the most important thing in life to me was fame and fortune.

But then it all changed. I asked God to help me get on the "right track" and He began changing my attitude. This newfound freedom enabled me to forgive myself and others, be kinder to people, and be positive no matter what the circumstance. I found a key ingredient to happy living: focusing more on others and less on myself,

I was no longer obsessed with winning at all costs. I also found out firsthand that staying in the race and not giving up — like the brave example set by Derek Redmond, and other sports heroes I've mentioned — is what all of us need to do when obstacles are against us and the going gets tough. Remember: **Life isn't always about winning the race; life is about finishing the race.** How many people can you help finish the race? In the end it may be you who needs a helping hand.

Remember, the greatest risk is not taking one!

Part of getting back up, is being willing to take "good risks." Don't be afraid to take chances or fall in love again. Along the way, you'll have your heart broken and you'll break others' hearts. You'll fight with your best friend; you'll cry because people you love won't love you back; and people you love dearly have been or will be taken from you. But through the storms, God gives us a beautiful rainbow. To find true happiness, you must find peace within yourself and let go of the hurt. You must get back up. After that, you'll be free to love again.

Suffering the loss of my family members was definitely my test in getting back up. But it took me a while to figure out that a lot of my sufferings were of my own making. I look back on my life and realize I made some terrible mistakes. I've hurt people with my attitude, and I've hurt myself and others with my addictions. Things would make me angry, or I'd lose control because I wasn't happy with the person I had become. This negative self-perception resulted in broken dreams and broken relationships.

As I shared before, I thought the way to happiness was through fame and fortune. And I always had to have things "my way." The sad truth is that when I did have money and things my way, I still wasn't happy. I was a slave to my desires.

I know I can never go back and change anything that happened, and I can't change any of the choices I've made. For that I am truly sorry to anyone I ever hurt or offended… especially my family. But I can change my future choices. And I can learn from my mistakes.

Never stop believing that good things can come out of negative situations. Every new day is another chance to change your life. If you've erred in your ways, forgive yourself. We can't change our past, nor can we run from it. But if we learn and grow from it, we can have an awesome future.

If you can look up, you can get up!

Like me, you too can reinvent yourself. That's what I did eight years ago when I surrendered my will to choose God's best for me. Sometimes it's hard to relate to that person I was in 2003. Trust me… there were many times I was at the end of my rope and just wanted to give up. But through my faith and belief, God gave me a little more slack — or what the Bible refers to as "Grace." I asked God for a "do-over," and He granted my wish.

Though I'm not proud of my past mistakes, I am honestly thankful for everything I've gone through in my life. Even my bad choices became valuable learning experiences. Yesterday shapes us into who we are today; God's amazing grace gives us the boost to climb out of the pit — and begin to live life to the fullest!

Maybe you've made a bad choice that cost you your dream or a relationship. You have the opportunity to start over, to make changes in your life. As I did, you can learn from your mistakes, overcome your hardships, correct your choices, and get back up.

It's never too late to rewrite your life story. Sometimes it takes a little longer to be the person God destined you to be. I am just thankful for my second chances. Give yourself permission to have another go at life. After all, failing is not getting knocked down… failure is simply giving up the fight. You *can* get back up… you can be a winner. I *believe* in you!

From my darkest moment… to New Life.

So how did I get a second chance? How did I rise up from where I was to where I am now? I will forever remember that very day in 2003 when my life changed. I was spiraling out of control. My body was broken from drug abuse and eight surgeries, and my heart was broken from the loss of parents, siblings, and my ex-wife. I was definitely at the low point of my life. As I mentioned, I spent that Christmas at the pier in Cocoa Beach, Florida, watching the waves roll in and out, contemplating the end. I remember feeling like I didn't want to be here anymore.

Have you ever felt like you couldn't go on anymore? Did you ever feel unappreciated and unloved? I was so depressed. I was once on top of the world; I had it all… fame, fortune, family. And suddenly I found myself empty, with nothing. I just wanted out!

How much can a heart take? I came home one night and retrieved my handgun from the nightstand next to my bed. When I opened the drawer an adrenaline rush soared through me. Then I walked into the shower and placed the cold, hard pistol to my head. I leaned against the smooth glass wall, calculating my next step. My plan was to slide down the wall slowly, and when I hit the ground, I would pull the trigger.

But as I started to descend, I got a vision of Hell. It was the most scared I had ever felt. I didn't want to spend eternity in that horrible place. I didn't want to be separated from God, and family that passed before me.

The tallest I have ever stood was when I got down on my knees.

It was at this point I got down on my knees and asked God to forgive me, to give me direction, to give me strength, and help me do His will. I experienced my own resurrection through faith. God gave me the ability to press the RESET BUTTON on Life — and I accepted His divine "Gift." God gives each one of us that chance! I recommitted my life to Him. God gave me joy and hope that is eternal; He gave me a peace this world doesn't offer — peace that surpasses understanding! And because I know He loves me, I trust my Heavenly Father.

Thankfully, I'm still here today. I am a survivor — a living example of what people can go through and miraculously achieve. Not only did I endure, I transformed. I changed my ways. I changed my choices.

The secret to victorious living can be yours.

I am no different than anyone else. People say "Marc, you're always so happy, you're always in a good mood." Please know it isn't like bad things don't happen to me. I have to deal with the same economy as everyone else. Some days I wake up on the wrong side of the bed, too. God did not make me perfect… I still make mistakes.

Like you, I have problems I have to figure out every day. Like you, I was a small child once with dreams. Like you, I first crawled, then I walked, then I ran. I'm still moving forward. As the self-proclaimed "Happiest Person on the Planet," I have a purpose and a mission. Every day is a miracle and I now appreciate life with a whole new outlook.

The greatest decision I ever made was accepting Jesus Christ as my Lord and Savior.

I don't believe it is a coincidence you're reading this book. Maybe it's time to strike up a friendship with God, to build a stronger relationship with Him today, to recommit your life. If you have never accepted Christ as your personal Savior, you can do it right now. What must you do? First, you must realize you cannot save yourself. Romans 3:23 teaches that *all have sinned and fall short of the glory of God.* Being a "good person" is not enough in the eyes of our Holy Creator.

Ephesians 2:8-9: *For it is by grace you have been saved, through faith — and this not from yourselves, it is the gift of God — not by works, so that no one can boast.* He sent Jesus to make up for our shortcomings. Because of Jesus we can become "perfect" in God's eyes.

One day we will all stand before God and give an account of our life.

2 Corinthians 5:10: *For we must all appear before the judgment seat of Christ, that each one may receive what is due him for the things done while in the body, whether good or bad.*

God wants us to be prepared. From reading God's word we can surmise we will be asked these questions: "What did you do with my Son Jesus Christ?" Did you accept him as your Lord and Savior? If so, "what did you do with your life?" The gifts He gave us. Did we spend them on ourselves or did we do God's will? The first question determines where you will spend eternity, and the second question will determine what rewards you will receive in eternity. Are you ready?

It starts with a prayer. Why not call on the Lord in repentance and faith and surrender right now?

With a sincere heart, embrace the gift of Salvation that God provides. If you are ready to take this exciting next step, then pray this prayer with me.

Heavenly Father:
I come to You in prayer asking for the forgiveness of
my Sins. I confess with my mouth and believe with my
heart that Jesus is your Son, and that he died on the
Cross at Calvary that I might be forgiven and have
Eternal Life in the Kingdom of Heaven.
Father, I believe that Jesus rose from the dead
and I ask You right now to come in to my life
and be my personal Lord and Savior.
I repent of my Sins and will Worship You, Lord, all the
days of my Life! Because your Word is Truth.
In Jesus' Name, Amen.

If you prayed this prayer, congratulations! You've taken the first step to being truly happy. On your new journey I encourage you to find a Bible-believing church in your area. Become active, read the Bible, and surround yourself with other Christians so you will grow in your faith. Above all, enjoy the freedom of knowing you are loved and cherished beyond measure — a precious child of God who will live forever!

POZ Pointers

❖ Accept the past, and "grow" from it.
❖ Forgive yourself and forgive others.
❖ Maintain an attitude of gratitude.
❖ Seek God and trust Him to handle the future.

Chapter Nine: Believe the best is YET to come.

*Y*our adventure is just beginning! If you have faith in God, dream BIG, Think POZ, and "do the right thing," the BEST is yet to come! We all go through hard times in life. In an early chapter I emphasized how we don't know what we have until we lose it. It's also true that we don't know what we've been missing until it arrives — like my precious wife, Darlene.

My point is that unexpected blessings can be right around the corner... so never give up hope. Today is a treasured gift! It is important to cherish every moment, because tomorrow might not ever come. This does not mean we should live recklessly; but rather, righteously... making wise choices.

In chapter seven I talked about how important it is to "let it go." Every time you allow a negative thought to enter your mind, fight it with Faith and believe that the future holds a promise for you. Even though you may not think so, we all have a purpose. God ordered the universe. He put you here for a specific time and reason.

In the book of Ecclesiastics, Solomon said there is a "*time for every purpose under Heaven.*" The place God calls you to may be different from what you think you need, want or expect. Have faith and ask for guidance. The times and the places may change, but God's divine purpose and His plans are perfectly mapped out like the stars in Heaven.

If you don't already know what your purpose is, ask the God who created you. Seek the wisdom of those "POZ people" around you. Keep listening to your heart, your good conscience, supportive friends or family, and God's voice — then follow that calling!

Ask yourself: What is it I really WANT to do in life? What do I do WELL, or have a desire to ACHIEVE? Based on your insights, wisdom from trusted sources, and prayer, choose worthwhile goals and set priorities. Without purpose, life loses its zest. We simply go through the motions — we eat, exercise, go to school or work, and wake up one day wondering what's it all for? We wander along without clear direction, maybe mix with the wrong crowd, get addicted to unhealthy habits, and perhaps end up identifying ourselves through our school activities or our job.

How many times have you gone to a party, and people ask what you do? We say, "I'm a nurse," or "I'm an honors student," or a "business major." We seldom say, "I'm a great leader," or "I'm a great Son" or "I'm the happiest person on the planet." Start thinking of yourself in a new way. I remember how I used to answer that question: "I'm a heavy weight champion." Now, I response with, "I'm a champion of choices!"

If you study successful people, you'll find they take the time to understand who they are and to find out what they're supposed to be doing. And they treat what they find as a treasure. You never hear them say, "Dang, I could never do that!" They honor their purpose by giving it their best shot and following where it leads.

As the saying goes, there are three types of people in this world: those who make things happen, those who watch things happen, and those who wonder what happened. Which one do you want to be? We all have a choice. I choose to make things happen. I choose to be happy — "the happiest person on the planet."

The discovery of God's true purpose in my life has brought peace and fulfillment. My new happiness has nothing to do with anything material. For starters, I have a new family. Christmas, birthdays, and other holidays have never been more splendid.

God has shown me how precious life is, and I will never again take my blessings for granted. I will spend my life giving back, "making someone's day." I am happy because God is using me to help change peoples' lives for the better. I am humbled... I am privileged. I can think of nothing more impactful than contributing to someone else's happiness.

Paul graduating from Rollins College

Let your success be measured by the joy in your heart. When I leave this earth, I want my achievements to simply be that I did God's will, not my own — that I was faithful to my wife and family, that I fought for what was right, that I had compassion for people in need. Whether I have one day or 100 years left, I want to live every day happy, positive, and productive. You can too!

This is the day your life really begins.

Congratulations... You've taken that important first step by reading this book. Now take action toward a new beginning. Your life stretches gloriously before you, and it's an amazing journey. Strike that balance in appreciating the small things along the way while believing the best is still yet to come.

Use your God-given talents to live life to the fullest. Make every day a victory! Be a better friend, co-worker, spouse, mother or father, son or daughter, or a better sibling. Forgive everyone and everything! Tell someone what they mean to you; speak up for what you believe in; dance even if you don't know how (like me!).

Seek joy. Hold someone's hand, comfort a friend, stay up late, be spontaneous, fall asleep holding the one you love, and smile until your face hurts. I am fully engaged in life, and I can't wait to start each new day. I am as prepared to die as I am prepared to live. Every moment I appreciate because I know it's an opportunity to make a difference. You can make a difference too! You're now on the journey to being the happiest person on the planet!

What's next? Staying in touch!

If my book has encouraged or helped you become a happier person, please write and tell me about it. As I meet thousands of people around the world, there's nothing I enjoy more than hearing about the transformation in their lives. I'd like to know about your journey. Connect with me at **www.ThinkPoz.org**. And be sure to check out my "POZ Thoughts" on Facebook at **www.facebook.com/marcmero2**

May you discover your purpose in life, devote yourself to God's will, and choose to be "The Happiest Person on the Planet!"

The King of POZ

CPSIA information can be obtained at www.ICGtesting.com
Printed in the USA
LVOW040933230512

282930LV00003B/2/P